POISON!
THE SPITTING COBRA
AND OTHER VENOMOUS ANIMALS

Greg Roza

PowerKiDS press
New York

Published in 2011 by The Rosen Publishing Group, Inc.
29 East 21st Street, New York, NY 10010

First Edition

Editor: Jennifer Way
Book Design: Kate Laczynski

Photo Credits: Cover, pp. 1, 4, 5 (top), 17 (top), 20–21 Shutterstock.com; pp. 5 (bottom), 10, 13, 15 iStockphoto/Thinkstock; p. 6, 7 Joe McDonald/Getty Images; p. 8 Gary Vestal/Getty Images; p. 9 Bruce Dale/Getty Images; p. 11 Emanuele Biggi/Getty Images; p. 12 Digital Vision/Thinkstock; pp. 14, 17 (bottom) Hemera/Thinkstock; p. 16 Jupiterimages/Photos.com/Thinkstock; p. 18 Tim Laman/Getty Images; p. 19 Jason Edwards/Getty Images; p. 22 Steve Morenos/Newspix/Getty Images.

Library of Congress Cataloging-in-Publication Data

Roza, Greg.
 Poison! : the spitting cobra and other venomous animals / by Greg Roza. — 1st ed.
   p. cm. — (Armed and dangerous)
 Includes index.
 ISBN 978-1-4488-2550-9 (library binding) — ISBN 978-1-4488-2684-1 (pbk.) —
ISBN 978-1-4488-2685-8 (6-pack)
 1. Poisonous animals—Juvenile literature. 2. Spitting cobras—Juvenile literature. I. Title.
 QL100.R694 2011
 591.6'5—dc22

                                    2010027074

Manufactured in the United States of America

CPSIA Compliance Information: Batch #WW11PK: For Further Information contact Rosen Publishing, New York, New York at 1-800-237-9932

CONTENTS

ARMED WITH VENOM!

Have you ever been stung by a bee? Have you ever wondered why bee stings hurt so much? Bees use their stingers to shoot **venom** into your body. Venom is a kind of poison that some animals' bodies produce. Bee venom causes itching, pain, and swelling.

Bees are not the only animals that use venom to

The spitting cobra, shown here, is a venomous snake. Like other cobras, the spitting cobra spreads the skin around its neck to form a hood. This hood is meant to warn animals that the snake is ready to strike to protect itself.

attack or **defend** themselves. Bee venom is very weak compared to the venom of other animals. The world is filled with animals armed with venom, from snakes to bugs to fish. The animals in this book use venom to stop **predators** and catch **prey**.

Scorpion fish are a family of venomous fish. The spines on their bodies are coated with venom.

5

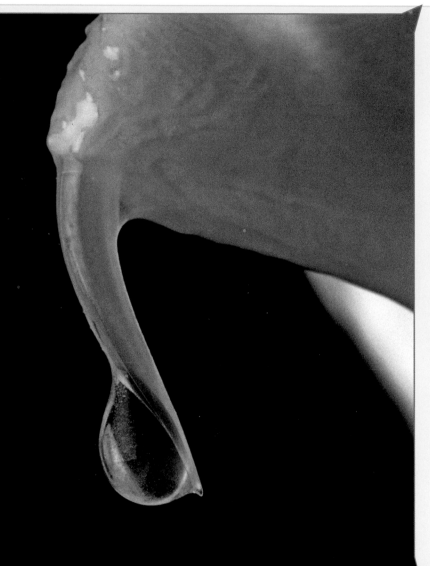

Venomous animals have different ways of using venom. Most use a sharp stinger, claw, or tooth to **inject** venom into their enemies. A bee's stinger, for example, **pierces** an animal's skin and shoots venom into it. The venom mixes with the animal's blood and is carried

Here you can see a drop of venom on a venomous snake's fang.

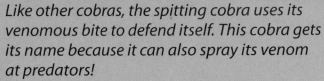

Like other cobras, the spitting cobra uses its venomous bite to defend itself. This cobra gets its name because it can also spray its venom at predators!

throughout its body. The venom can then have a number of different effects on the animal.

A few animals have more interesting ways of using venom. The spitting cobra, for example, shoots venom at its enemies. This snake is very good at hitting its enemies in the eyes!

IN THE BLOOD

An animal's blood carries venom throughout its body. Different venoms affect the body in different ways. Some, like bee venom, are weak. These venoms cause itching, swelling, and pain. Other venoms do much greater harm. Strong venoms can cause difficulty breathing, difficulty

Eastern diamondback rattlesnakes also use their fangs to hunt prey. They eat mice, rats, squirrels, and birds.

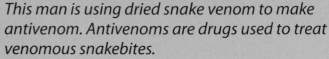
This man is using dried snake venom to make antivenom. Antivenoms are drugs used to treat venomous snakebites.

moving, heart failure, and even death.

The eastern diamondback rattlesnake is the largest venomous snake in the United States. Its bite is both painful and deadly. This snake's venom harms the blood and kills **tissue**. Someone who is bitten by a diamondback must take a drug right away to stop the venom.

DEFEND AND ATTACK

Some animals use venom to defend themselves when they feel they are in danger. Stingrays, for example, like to rest on the seabed near shore. If someone scares or steps on the stingray, it will attack using the stinger on its tail. Its venom causes pain, which gives it time to get away.

Others animals use venom while hunting. Tarantulas attack just about any animal

The end of a stingray's tail has a sharp stinger. The stinger has venom in it. Stingrays use their stingers to defend themselves.

This tarantula has used its sharp fangs to hunt. It used its venom to kill a frog, which it is now eating.

smaller than them. Some even attack small birds and lizards! A tarantula uses its sharp **fangs** to inject a powerful venom into its prey. After the venom kills the prey, the tarantula begins to eat it.

SPITTING COBRA

Most venomous snakes use their fangs to inject venom. The spitting cobra can inject venom with its fangs, or it can spit its venom. However, this cobra does not really spit its venom the way you might

The spitting cobra's venom does not harm an animal if it hits only skin. However, the spitting cobra is very good at aiming for a predator's eyes!

Spitting cobras eat all kinds of small animals. They eat mice, other snakes, and birds, such as the lilac-breasted roller shown here. They also eat the eggs of many animals.

think. It sprays the venom out of its fangs. It can hit a moving animal up to 10 feet (3 m) away.

The spitting cobra has an amazing ability to hit its enemy in the eyes almost every time. The cobra guesses where a moving enemy's eyes will be, and then it lets the venom fly! The venom causes pain and sometimes blindness.

SCORPION FISH

The scorpion fish is a venomous animal. It has a bumpy body and brown coloring, which makes the scorpion fish good at hiding near rocks and plants. It uses this **camouflage** to hide from its prey, which it snaps up in its large mouth.

Scorpion fish have fins with venomous points. They do not use them for hunting. They use them to scare away

This scorpion fish is camouflaged among the rocks on the seafloor. Its mouth is open and waiting for prey to swim by.

The lionfish, shown here, is part of the scorpion fish family. You can see the venomous spikes sticking out from its body.

enemies. Divers need to be very careful when they are close to the seafloor because they can get stung by scorpion fish. A scorpion fish sting is very painful.

Divers can get a painful scorpion fish sting if they do not look out for these venomous fish.

GILA MONSTER

The Gila monster is a lizard. Adults can grow up to be 2 feet (61 cm) long. They are somewhat fat and lazy! They spend most of their time sleeping underground or lying in the sun.

Gila monsters chew on their prey until their venom kills the animal. This Gila monster is almost done eating its dinner!

The Gila monster can inject a painful venom with its teeth. It uses this venom to defend itself and to catch food. The Gila monster does not just bite once, it holds on and chews! As the Gila monster chews on an animal, its venom flows into the animal's blood. The venom is strong enough to kill a small animal or hurt a larger animal.

Gila monsters eat small animals, such as the desert pygmy mouse shown here.

PLATYPUS

The platypus is one of the strangest animals on Earth. Do not let the platypus's looks fool you, though. You might be surprised to learn it is venomous, too.

Male platypuses have stingers on each of their back feet. They use these stingers to defend themselves.

Platypuses are strange-looking animals! They have bills that look like ducks' and tails that look like beavers'.

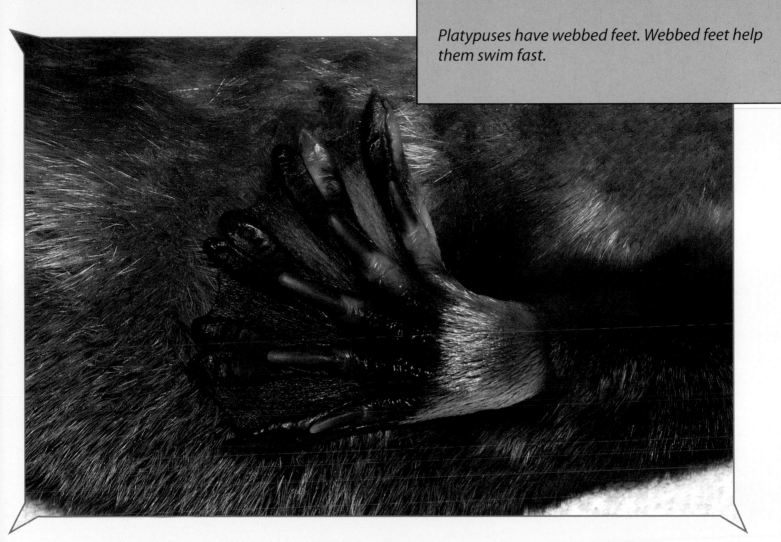

Platypuses have webbed feet. Webbed feet help them swim fast.

They may also use them to fight other male platypuses. The venom is very painful and is strong enough to kill a small dog. An adult platypus is only about the size of a cat, but its venom is strong enough to make even big predators want to stay away.

FUN FACTS

1 A scientist named Bruce Young studied how the spitting cobra defends itself. To do this, he wore a clear cover over his face and let a cobra spit venom at his eyes!

2 Like most cobras, the spitting cobra forms a hood when it is scared. The cobra flattens the part of its body below its head to make itself look bigger.

3 There are more than a dozen kinds of spitting cobras found in Africa and Australia.

4 Scorpion fish venom can cause pain, swelling, difficulty breathing, and more serious effects. However, some people keep them as pets!

The Gila monster is one of two types of venomous lizards found in the southwestern United States and Mexico. It is also the largest lizard in the United States.

5

Platypuses are one of only two venomous mammals in the world.

6

The box jellyfish has the strongest venom of any sea animal. One sting can kill a person.

7

PEOPLE AND VENOM

There are many venomous animals in the world, and sometimes these animals attack people. Most of the time they do this because a person has surprised or hurt the animal.

There are different ways to treat people who have been bitten or stung. There are drugs to treat many

types of snake and spider bites. With the most powerful venom, the person bitten needs to take the drug right away or he or she could die. Even the weakest bee venom makes some people very sick. They must carry a drug with them in case they are ever stung by a bee.

GLOSSARY

camouflage (KA-muh-flahj) A color or shape that matches what is around something and helps hide it.

defend (dih-FEND) To guard from harm.

fangs (FANGZ) Sharp teeth that inject venom.

inject (in-JEKT) To use a sharp object to force something into a body.

pierces (PEERS-ez) Makes a hole in something.

predators (PREH-duh-ters) Animals that kill other animals for food.

prey (PRAY) An animal that is hunted by another animal for food.

tissue (TIH-shoo) Matter that forms the parts of living things.

venom (VEH-num) A poison passed by one animal into another through a bite or a sting.

INDEX

WEB SITES

Due to the changing nature of Internet links, PowerKids Press has developed an online list of Web sites related to the subject of this book. This site is updated regularly. Please use this link to access the list:
www.powerkidslinks.com/armd/poison/